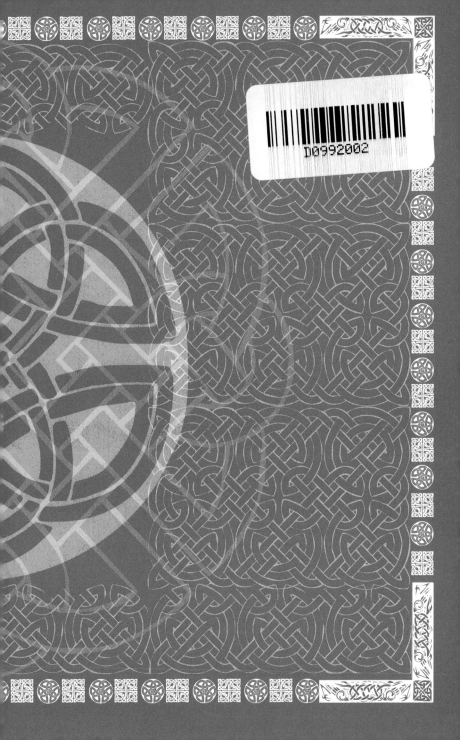

A Terrible Beauty

Mairéad Ashe FitzGerald is the author of
*Thomas Johnson Westropp (1860–1922) An Irish
Antiquary*, *Exploring the World of Colmcille*, and
Best-Loved Yeats.

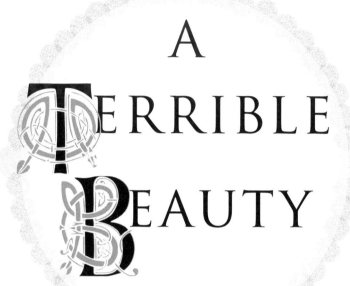

A TERRIBLE BEAUTY

POETRY OF 1916

selected by
MAIRÉAD ASHE FITZGERALD

Illustrations & Design by Emma Byrne

THE O'BRIEN PRESS
DUBLIN

First published 2015 by The O'Brien Press Ltd.
12 Terenure Road East, Rathgar, Dublin 6, D06 HD27, Ireland.
Tel: +353 1 4923333; Fax: +353 1 4922777
E-mail: books@obrien.ie; Website: www.obrien.ie
Reprinted 2016.

ISBN: 978-1-84717-359-1

10 9 8 7 6 5 4 3 2
20 19 18 17 16

Cover illustration: Emma Byrne
Printed and bound in Poland by Białostockie Zakłady Graficzne S.A.
The paper in this book is produced using pulp from managed forests.

Every effort has been made to trace copyright holders and to obtain their per-
mission for the use of copyright material. The publisher apologises for any
errors or omissions and would be grateful if notified of any corrections that
should be incorporated in future reprints or editions of this book.

ACKNOWLEDGEMENTS

Sincere thanks to the Librarian and staff of the Library of the Royal Irish Academy and also to the staff at Special Collections in University College Dublin for their generous assistance and for allowing access to their unique material.

The editor and publisher gratefully acknowledge permission to include the following copyright material:

Bax, Arnold (Dermot O'Byrne): 'A Dublin Ballad—1916', 'Martial Law in Dublin', 'Shells at Oranmore'. The poems are reproduced by permission of the Bax Estate and are copyright.

Colum, Padraic: 'The Rebel. Roger Casement, 1864–1916'. By kind permission of the Estate of Padraic Colum.

O'Casey, Seán: 'Thomas Ashe' © The Estate of Seán O'Casey. By kind permission of the Estate of Seán O'Casey, care of Macnaughton Lord Representation of 44 South Molton Street, London, W1K 5RT.

Stephens, James: 'Spring—1916'. Reproduced by permission of The Society of Authors as the literary representatives of the Estate of James Stephens.

TABLE OF CONTENTS

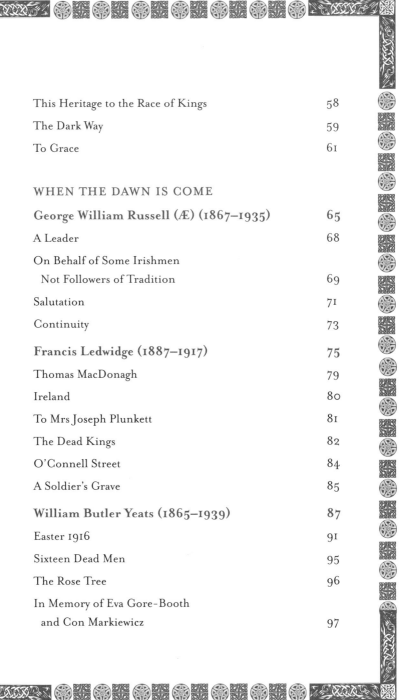

AFTERMATH & REQUIEM

A COUNTRY'S AWAKENING

The trauma of the Great Famine had left Ireland with a fractured society and a culture on the verge of extinction. The drain of emigration, the near demise of the Irish language, alongside the erosion of modes of thought and knowledge from past generations were causing a slow death for a national culture.

However, by the end of the nineteenth century improved literacy, more secure land tenure and an increased politicisation of the people had led to a reawakening of a sense of Irishness. The stage was set for a life-giving movement inspired by a new generation of Irish people – people of vision and energy, idealists who found a cause in saving and promoting Irish culture. There was a prevailing atmosphere of renewal and youth which brought a revitalised energy to the Irish language, the visual arts, literature, the theatre and the sporting arena. A new enthusiasm for the ancient Gaelic games of football and hurling was generated with the foundation of the Gaelic Athletic Association in 1884; the Gaelic League was founded by Douglas Hyde, Eoin MacNeill and others with the purpose of restoring and promoting Irish language and culture; Irish music was celebrated through the Feis Ceoil, founded in 1897. The glories of early Celtic art found a new life under the momentum of the Irish Arts and Crafts movement; this was expressed in the works of artists such as Sarah Purser, who established the stained-glass studio of An Túr Gloine, and in the various artistic enterprises of the Yeats sisters.

While WB Yeats and Lady Gregory were committed to founding a national theatre, Dublin was full of theatres run by the young. Pádraic Pearse, Thomas MacDonagh and Joseph Mary Plunkett, whose poetic works are included in this book, were all engaged in theatrical pursuits: writing and staging plays, and founding theatres and literary journals. All three were poets and writers and, like many of their associates, they were engaged in every aspect of the cultural revival.

Poetry had a long history of living underground in the Gaelic tradition, and dreams of nationhood and the longing for freedom found expression in a particular way in poetry. Little wonder, then, that the same three poets, Pearse, MacDonagh and Plunkett, were among those who walked out on Easter Monday morning 1916 to set their country free. Their poetry expresses that longing for freedom that the authorities, fully taken up with parliamentarian and rebel movements, were blind to.

In the aftermath of the Rising, the executions of the leaders and their callous burial without ceremony in a mass grave* generated an outpouring of poetry. Written by almost every poet who took part in the literary revival, these poems, many of which are placed in this collection, gave words to the depth of anger, pride, grief and identity growing amongst the people.

The Rising was a glorious failure, but a people was awakening to the possibilities of nationhood, and the transforming events of Easter 1916 were immortalised by the poet WB Yeats: 'All changed, changed utterly, a terrible beauty is born.'

* Fourteen of the leaders were buried in a mass grave at Arbour Hill in Dublin. Thomas Kent was executed in Cork and buried in the grounds of Cork Prison. Roger Casement was hanged in Pentonville Prison in London in August 1916, and buried in quicklime.

THE CONFLUENCE

OF DREAMS

PÁDRAIC PEARSE

(1879–1916)

The son of an English father and an Irish
mother, Pádraic Pearse (Pádraic Mac Piarais)
was born in what was then Great Brunswick
Street (now Pearse Street) in Dublin in 1879.
Passionately devoted to Irish culture, he joined the
newly formed Gaelic League in 1895, at seventeen,
and went on to become editor of its newspaper,
An Claidheamh Soluis, in 1903. He believed that
Ireland could only attain a true identity and lasting
independence through a revived Irish language and
literature which had been nearly destroyed due to
famine, emigration and a hostile education system.

Founding St Enda's School for boys and St Ita's for
girls saw Pearse in his role as gifted and reforming
educationalist. His belief in the importance of the
arts and creativity attracted the young, the talented,
those looking for a cause, to teach in his schools,
amongst them his brother, Willie Pearse, a sculptor

and actor; Thomas MacDonagh, a poet and future leader in the 1916 Rising; Mary Maguire Colum, a writer and critic; and teacher Louise Gavan Duffy, who spent Easter Week in the General Post Office (GPO) during the Rising. Pearse's choice of the beautiful surroundings of The Hermitage in Rathfarnham for St Enda's was part of this philosophy and attracted other like-minded idealists. Artists such as Sarah Purser, Jack B Yeats and Beatrice Elvery gave paintings. WB Yeats, Douglas Hyde, Edward Martyn, George Moore, the poets Joseph Campbell and Padraic Colum, and Máire Nic Shiubhlaigh of the Abbey Theatre visited the school, gave lectures and attended the plays put on by the pupils. It was a place where cultural nationalism flourished.

Pearse's own writings poured out of St Enda's: translations of poems from Irish, stories such as *Íosagán agus Scéalta Eile* and dramas and essays. Pearse had a deep and scholarly knowledge of Gaelic literature and translated numerous poems from the early modern period by poets such as Geoffrey Keating (Seathrún Céitinn), Piaras Feiritéar and others. He wrote extensively on the subject of education and his essay entitled *The Murder Machine* was widely influential. Pearse also gradually became prominent in revolutionary circles and moved towards a more military position. He was a founder-member of the Irish Volunteers in 1913 and was a member of the Irish Republican Brotherhood (IRB).

The public platform suited Pearse; he had a growing reputation for eloquence and leadership. He was chosen by Thomas Clarke to give what was an electrifying and oft-quoted oration over the grave of the old Fenian Jeremiah O'Donovan Rossa in Glasnevin Cemetery in August 1915:

> They think that they have pacified Ireland. They think that they have pacified half of us and intimidated the other half. They think that they have foreseen everything, think that they have provided against everything; but the fools, the fools, the fools! they have left us our Fenian dead, and while Ireland holds these graves, Ireland unfree shall never be at peace.
>
> *Extract from Pearse's speech over the grave of*
> *Jeremiah O'Donovan Rossa in Glasnevin Cemetery.*

Pearse played a central role in the IRB planning of the coming insurrection. The courage and leadership that he displayed as commander-in-chief in the GPO determined to a great extent the course of events of that fateful week. The Rising ultimately ended in surrender on Saturday, 29 April. Pearse was held in Arbour Hill Barracks, away from his comrades, from Saturday until Tuesday, 2 May, when he was brought to Richmond Barracks for court martial. He spoke from the dock and was given the death sentence, which he received with characteristic composure. A writer to the last, Pearse spent the hours before his death in Kilmainham Jail leaving instructions for his literary affairs and composing some final letters to his family and his last poem, 'The Wayfarer'. He was executed by firing squad at dawn on Wednesday, 3 May. The poems selected here reflect the range of Pearse's poetry, some of which he wrote in Irish with translations in English. They show the spirit of self-sacrifice and renunciation that informed his life's work, and most of all, the soul of the rebel who so desired to see his country freed.

THE REBEL

I am come of the seed of the people, the people that sorrow,
That have no treasure but hope,
No riches laid up but a memory
Of an Ancient glory.
My mother bore me in bondage, in bondage my mother
was born,
I am of the blood of serfs;
The children with whom I have played, the men and
women with whom I have eaten,
Have had masters over them, have been under the lash of
masters,
And, though gentle, have served churls;
The hands that have touched mine, the dear hands whose
touch is familiar to me,
Have worn shameful manacles, have been bitten at the
wrist by manacles,
Have grown hard with the manacles and the task-work
of strangers,
I am flesh of the flesh of these lowly, I am bone of their
bone,
I that have never submitted;
I that have a soul greater than the souls of my people's
masters,
I that have vision and prophecy and the gift of fiery speech,
I that have spoken with God on the top of His holy hill.

And because I am of the people, I understand the people,
I am sorrowful with their sorrow, I am hungry with their
   desire:
My heart has been heavy with the grief of mothers,
My eyes have been wet with the tears of children.
I have yearned with old wistful men,
And laughed or cursed with young men;
Their shame is my shame, and I have reddened for it,
Reddened for that they have served, they who should
   be free,
Reddened for that they have gone in want, while others
   have been full,
Reddened for that they have walked in fear of lawyers
   and of their jailers
With their writs of summons and their handcuffs,
Men mean and cruel!
I could have borne stripes on my body rather than this
   shame of my people.

And now I speak, being full of vision;
I speak to my people, and I speak in my people's name to
   the masters of my people.
I say to my people that they are holy, that they are august,
   despite their chains,
That they are greater than those that hold them, and
   stronger and purer,
That they have but need of courage, and to call on the
   name of their God,

God the unforgetting, the dear God that loves the peoples
For whom He died naked, suffering shame.
And I say to my people's masters: Beware,
Beware of the thing that is coming, beware of the risen
 people,
Who shall take what ye would not give. Did ye think
 to conquer the people,
Or that Law is stronger than life and than men's desire to
 be free?
We will try it out with you, ye that have harried and held,
Ye that have bullied and bribed, tyrants, hypocrites, liars!

FORNOCHT DO CHONAC THÚ

Fornocht do chonac thú,
A áille na háille,
Is do dhallas mo shúil
Ar eagla go stánfainn.

Do chualas do cheol,
A bhinne na binne,
Is do dhúnas mo chluas
Ar eagla go gclisfinn.

Do bhlaiseas do bhéal,
A mhilse na milse,
Is chruas mo chroí
Ar eagla mo mhillte.

Do dhallas mo shúil,
Is mo chluas do dhúnas,
Do chruas mo chroí
Is mo mhian do mhúchas;

Do thugas mo chúl
Ar an aisling a chumas,
'S ar an ród seo romham
M'aghaidh do thugas.

Do thugas mo ghnúis
Ar an ród seo romham,
Ar an ngníomh do-chím,
'S ar an mbás do-gheobhad.

RENUNCIATION

Naked I saw thee,
O beauty of beauty,
And I blinded my eyes
For fear I should fail.

I hear thy music,
O melody of melody,
And I closed my ears
For fear I should falter.

I tasted thy mouth,
O sweetness of sweetness,
And I hardened my heart
For fear of my slaying.

I blinded my eyes,
And I closed my ears,
I hardened my heart
And I smothered my desire.

I turned my back
On the vision I had shaped,
And to this road before me
I turned my face.

I have turned my face
To this road before me,
To the deed that I see
And the death I shall die.

THE FOOL

Since the wise men have not spoken, I speak that am
  only a fool;
A fool that hath loved his folly,
Yea, more than the wise men their books or their counting
  houses, or their quiet homes,
Or their fame in men's mouths;
A fool that in all his days hath done never a prudent thing,
Never hath counted the cost, nor recked if another reaped
The fruit of his mighty sowing, content to scatter the seed;
A fool that is unrepentant, and that soon at the end of all
Shall laugh in his lonely heart as the ripe ears fall to the
  reaping-hooks
And the poor are filled that were empty,
Tho' he go hungry.

I have squandered the splendid years that the Lord God
  gave to my youth
In attempting impossible things, deeming them alone
  worth the toil.
Was it folly or grace? Not men shall judge me, but God.

I have squandered the splendid years:
Lord, if I had the years I would squander them over again,
Aye, fling them from me!
For this I have heard in my heart, that a man shall scatter,
  not hoard,

Shall do the deed of to-day, nor take thought of to-morrow's teen,
Shall not bargain or huxter with God; or was it a jest of Christ's
And is this my sin before men, to have taken Him at His word?

The lawyers have sat in council, the men with the keen, long faces,
And said, 'This man is a fool,' and others have said,
    'He blasphemeth';
And the wise have pitied the fool that hath striven to give a life
In the world of time and space among the bulks of actual things,
To a dream that was dreamed in the heart, and that only the heart
    could hold.

O wise men, riddle me this: what if the dream come true?
What if the dream come true? and if millions unborn shall dwell
In the house that I shaped in my heart, the noble house of my
    thought?
Lord, I have staked my soul, I have staked the lives of my kin
On the truth of Thy dreadful word. Do not remember my failures,
But remember this my faith.

And so I speak.
Yea, ere my hot youth pass, I speak to my people and say:
Ye shall be foolish as I; ye shall scatter, not save;
Ye shall venture your all, lest ye lose what is more than all;
Ye shall call for a miracle, taking Christ at His word.
And for this I will answer, O people, answer here and hereafter,
O people that I have loved shall we not answer together?

MISE ÉIRE

Mise Éire:
Sine mé ná an Chailleach Bhéarra.

Mór mo ghlóir:
Mé a rug Cú Chulainn cróga.

Mór mo náir:
Mo chlann féin a dhíol a máthair.

Mise Éire:
Uaigní mé ná an Chailleach Bhéarra.

I AM IRELAND

(TRANSLATION OF MISE ÉIRE)

I am Ireland:
I am older than the old woman of Beare.

Great my glory:
I that bore Cuchulainn the valiant.

Great my shame:
My own children that sold their mother.

I am Ireland:
I am lonelier than the Old Woman of Beare.

THE MOTHER

I do not grudge them: Lord, I do not grudge
My two strong sons that I have seen go out
To break their strength and die, they and a few,
In bloody protest for a glorious thing,
They shall be spoken of among their people,
The generations shall remember them,
And call them blessed;
But I will speak their names to my own heart
In the long nights;
The little names that were familiar once
Round my dead hearth.
Lord, thou art hard on mothers:
We suffer in their coming and their going;
And tho' I grudge them not, I weary, weary
Of the long sorrow—And yet I have my joy:
My sons were faithful, and they fought.

THE WAYFARER

The beauty of the world hath made me sad,
This beauty that will pass;
Sometimes my heart hath shaken with great joy
To see a leaping squirrel in a tree,
Or a red lady-bird upon a stalk,
Or little rabbits in a field at evening,
Lit by a slanting sun,
Or some green hill where shadows drifted by
Some quiet hill where mountainy man hath sown
And soon would reap; near to the gate of Heaven;
Or children with bare feet upon the sands
Of some ebbed sea, or playing on the streets
Of little towns in Connacht,
Things young and happy.
And then my heart hath told me:
These will pass,
Will pass and change, will die and be no more,
Things bright and green, things young and happy;
And I have gone upon my way
Sorrowful.

Written by Pearse in Kilmainham Jail on the night before his execution.

THOMAS MACDONAGH

(1878—1916)

Thomas MacDonagh was born in 1878 in Cloughjordan, County Tipperary, where his parents were school teachers. He was educated at Rockwell College near Cashel, County Tipperary, by the Holy Ghost Fathers and studied there for the priesthood before moving to a teaching post in St Kieran's College, Kilkenny, in 1901. There he discovered the Gaelic League and immediately became swept up in the nationalist movement. Five years' teaching in St Colman's in Fermoy, County Cork, followed before MacDonagh moved to Dublin in 1908 to join Pádraic Pearse in St Enda's as assistant headmaster.

MacDonagh was blessed with a lighthearted personality, well suited to act as a foil to the seriousness of Pearse as headmaster. Padraic Colum called him 'a wonderfully good comrade, an eager friend, a happy-hearted companion' with 'a flow of wit and humour'. Together, MacDonagh and Pearse were a perfect team with shared interests: both were literary men and both were charismatic teachers with a love of poetry, theatre and the Irish language. MacDonagh was already well known in literary circles by the time he came to St Enda's. His play *When the Dawn is Come* (with its theme of Irish insurrection) was accepted by WB Yeats and Lady Gregory and staged in the Abbey Theatre in 1907. He had published three books of poetry by 1906. As early as 1903 he had sent some of his poems to WB Yeats, who responded with advice and encouragement. Yeats advised him to read and translate from Irish in order to fully experience the Irish mode of expression. Indeed, MacDonagh's translations, with their internal rhyme and assonance, beautifully preserve the fluidity and rhythm of the originals.

He read English, French and Irish at University College Dublin and became an inspired lecturer in the Department of English there. Thomas MacDonagh and Muriel Gifford were married in 1912 and they had two children, Donagh and Barbara. Muriel, who came from a Protestant Unionist family in Dublin, was an artist. Her sister was Grace Gifford, who was to marry Joseph Plunkett in Kilmainham Jail shortly before his execution.

MacDonagh was a literary innovator and critic, arguing for the individuality of national and cultural traditions. He made an immense contribution to the study and development of Irish literature in English. He believed that Irish writing must find a new separate identity in a time of transition, influenced by the Irish way of speech and by Irish music. His book *Literature in Ireland* is regarded as one of the most important works of literary criticism written in Ireland in the twentieth century. He was one of the founders of *The Irish Review*, an influential journal devoted to art and literature. He found time to act as manager to the Irish Theatre, which was founded by Joseph Plunkett and Edward Martyn.

By 1913, like Pearse, he was progressing from cultural nationalist to military separatist. With the founding of the Irish Volunteers in 1913, MacDonagh, a man of ideas and organisational competence, emerged as a natural leader. He became a member of the General Council and acted as director of training. He played a central role in planning for an insurrection, and Easter Monday 1916 saw him as commandant of a garrison in Jacob's Biscuit Factory, an enormous building in central Dublin. Máire Nic Shiubhlaigh, a great patriot, a member of Cumann na mBan and a renowned actress in the Abbey

Theatre, was in Jacob's Factory for the entire week of the Rising. She left a first-hand description of those events in her fine book, *The Splendid Years*, where she remembers MacDonagh's optimism and enthusiasm, giving encouragement to his garrison during the long hours and days of Easter Week. Dismayed by news of the surrender on Saturday, which only reached them on Sunday, MacDonagh was persuaded to meet with General Lowe and he and his comrades reluctantly laid down their arms. For his role in the Rising and his signature on the Proclamation, Thomas MacDonagh was tried by court martial at Kilmainham Jail and executed by firing squad on the morning of Wednesday, 3 May.

WISHES FOR MY SON

Born on Saint Cecilia's Day 1912

Now, my son, is life for you,
And I wish you joy of it,—
Joy of power in all you do,
Deeper passion, better wit
Than I had who had enough,
Quicker life and length thereof,
More of every gift but love.

Love I have beyond all men,
Love that now you share with me—
What have I to wish you then
But that you be good and free,
And that God to you may give
Grace in stronger days to live?

For I wish you more than I
Ever knew of glorious deed,
Though no rapture passed me by
That an eager heart could heed,
Though I followed heights and sought
Things the sequel never brought.

Wild and perilous holy things
Flaming with a martyr's blood,
And the joy that laughs and sings
Where a foe must be withstood,
Joy of headlong happy chance
Leading on the battle dance.

But I found no enemy,
No man in a world of wrong,
That Christ's word of charity
Did not render clean and strong—
Who was I to judge my kind,
Blindest groper of the blind?

God to you may give the sight
And the clear undoubting strength
Wars to knit for single right,
Freedom's war to knit at length,
And to win, through wrath and strife,
To the sequel of my life.

But for you, so small and young,
Born on Saint Cecilia's Day,
I in more harmonious song
Now for nearer joys should pray—
Simpler joys: the natural growth
Of your childhood and your youth,
Courage, innocence, and truth:

These for you, so small and young,
In your hand and heart and tongue.

OF A POET PATRIOT

His songs were a little phrase
Of eternal song,
Drowned in the harping of lays
More loud and long.

His deed was a single word,
Called out alone
In a night when no echo stirred
To laughter or moan.

But his songs new souls shall thrill,
The loud harps dumb,
And his deed the echoes fill
When the dawn is come.

AN BONNÁN BUÍ

BY CATHAL BUÍ MAC GIOLLA GUNNA

A bhonnáin bhuí, 'sé mo léan do luí
   Is do chnámha sínte tar éis do ghrinn,
Ní easpa bídh ach díobháil dí
   A d'fhág 'do luí thú ar chúl do chinn.
Is measa liom féin ná scrios na Traoí,
   Tú bheith gan bhrí ar leaca lom
Is nach ndearna tú díth ná dolaidh san tír
   Is nárbh fhearr leat fíon ná uisce poill.

A bhonnáin álainn, is é mo mhíle crá thú,
   Do chúl ar lár amuigh rómham sa tslí,
Is gurbh iomaí lá a chluininn do ghrág
   Ar an láib is tú ag ól na dí.
Is é an ní deir cách le do dheartháir Cathal
   Go bhfaighe sé bás mar siúd, má's fíor,
Ach ní hamhlaidh tá, siúd an préachán breá
   Chuaigh in éag ar ball le díth na dí.

A bhonnáin óig, is é mo mhíle brón
   Thú bheith sínte fuar i measc na dtonn
'S na luchaí móra ag trial chun do thorraimh
   Le déanamh spóirt agus pléisiúir ann;
Is dá gcuirfeá scéala fá mo dhéin-se
   Go raibh tú i ngéibhinn nó i mbroid gan bhrí,
Do bhrisfinn béim duit ar an loch sin Bhéasaigh
   A fhliuchfadh do bhéal is do chorp istigh.

Ní hiad bhur n-éanlaith atá mé ag éagnach,
   An lon, an smólach, ná an chorr ghlas
Ach mo bhonnán buí bhí lán de chroí,
   Is gur cosúil liom fein é i nós 's i ndath.
Bhíodh sé go síoraí ag ól na dí,
   Is deirtear go mbímse mar sin seal;
Nil braon dá bhaighinnse nach ligfinn sios
   Ar eagla go bhfaighinnse bás den tart!

Is é d'iarr mo stór orm ligean den ól,
   Nó nach mbeinnse beo ach seal beag gearr;
Ach dúirt mé léi go dtug sí an bhréag,
   Is gurbh fhada mo shaolsa an deoch úd a fháil;
An bhfaca sibh éan an phíopáin réidh
   A chuaigh in éag den tart ar ball?
Is a chomharsain chléibh, fliuchaidh bhur mbéal,
   Óir chan fhaigheann sibh braon i ndiaidh bhur mbáis!

THE YELLOW BITTERN

(TRANSLATION OF AN BONNÁN BUÍ
BY CATHAL BUÍ MAC GIOLLA GUNNA)

The yellow bittern that never broke out
   In a drinking bout, might as well have drunk;
His bones are thrown on a naked stone
   Where he lived alone like a hermit monk.
O yellow bittern! I pity your lot,
   Though they say that a sot like myself is curst—
I was sober a while, but I'll drink and be wise
   For I fear I should die in the end of thirst.

It's not for the common birds that I'd mourn,
   The black-bird, the corn-crake, or the crane,
But for the bittern that's shy and apart
   And drinks in the marsh from the lone bog-drain.
Oh! if I had known you were near your death,
   While my breath held out I'd have run to you,
Till a splash from the Lake of the Son of the Bird
   Your soul would have stirred and waked anew.

My darling told me to drink no more
   Or my life would be o'er in a little short while;
But I told her 'tis drink gives me health and strength
   And will lengthen my road by many a mile.
You see how the bird of the long smooth neck
   Could get his death from the thirst at last—
Come, son of my soul, and drain your cup,
   You'll get no sup when your life is past.

In a wintering island by Constantine's halls
   A bittern calls from a wineless place,
And tells me that hither he cannot come
   Till the summer is here and the sunny days.
When he crosses the stream there and wings o'er the sea
   Then a fear comes to me he may fail in his flight—
Well, the milk and the ale are drunk every drop,
   And a dram won't stop our thirst this night.

THE POET CAPTAIN

They called him their king, their leader of men, and he
  led them well
For one bright year and he vanquished their foe,
Breaking more battles than bards may tell,
Warring victoriously,—till the heart spake low
And said—Is it thus? Do not these things pass?
  What things abide?
They are but the birds from the ocean, the waves of the
  tide;
And thou art naught beside,—grass and a form of clay.
And said—The Ligurian fought in his day,—
In vain, in vain! Rome triumphs. He left his friends to
  the fight,
And their victory passed away,
And he like a star that flames and falls in the night.

But after another year they came to him again,
And said—Lead us forth again. Come with us again.
But still he answered them—You strive against fate in
  vain.
They said—Our race is old. We would not have it pass.
Ere Rome began we are, a gentle people of old,
Unsavage when all were wild.
And he—How Egypt was old in the days that were old,
Yet is passed, and we pass.
They said—We shall have striven, unreconciled.

And he went with them again, and they conquered again.
Till the same bare season closed his unquiet heart
To all but sorrow of life—This is in vain! Of yore
Lo, Egypt was, and all things do depart,
This is in vain! And he fought no more.

He conned the poems that poets had made in other days,
And he loved the past that he could pity and praise.
And he fought no more, living in solitude,
Till they came and called him back to the multitude,
Saying—Our olden speech and our old manners die.
He went again, and they raised his banner on high:
Came Victory, eagle-formed, with wings wide flung,
As with them a while he fought, with never a weary
    thought, and with never a sigh,
That their children might have again their manners and
    ancient tongue.

But again the sorrow of life whispered to his soul
And said—O little soul, striving to little goal!
Here is a finite world where all things change and change!
And said—In Mexico a people strange
Loved their manners and speech long ago when the world
    was young!
Their speech is silent long—What of it now?—Silent and
    dead

Their manners forgotten, and all but their memory sped!
And said—What matter? Heart will die and tongue;
Or if they live again they live in a place that is naught,
With other language, other custom, different thought.
He left them again to their fight, and no more for him they
    sought.
But they chose for leader a stern sure man
That looked not back on the waste of story:
For his country he fought in the battle's van,
And he won her peace and he won her glory.

JOSEPH MARY
PLUNKETT
(1887—1916)

oseph Mary Plunkett was born in 1887 into an affluent Dublin Catholic family at Upper Fitzwilliam Street. He grew up in a household with connections to the worlds of the arts and politics. His father was Count George Noble Plunkett, an art historian and a friend of Charles Stewart Parnell. The young Plunkett had a difficult childhood, plagued by tuberculosis and constant illness, as a result of which his schooling was erratic. He was a voracious reader and the two years (1906–1908) that he spent at the Jesuit College at Stonyhurst in Lancashire, England, gave him the ideal opportunity to study philosophy, mysticism, Egyptian archaeology as well as scientific subjects. It was clear from an early age that writing came easily to Plunkett; poetry, letters and diaries flowed from his pen. As a young man he was a seasoned traveller in Europe and spoke several languages. He spent six months in Algiers for his health. His travels made him an ideal person to undertake dangerous journeys to Europe and America on behalf of the Irish Volunteers when the Great War was under way.

In 1909 Plunkett met Thomas MacDonagh, who taught him Irish; the two had many interests in common and became firm friends. His first collection of poetry, *The Circle and the Sword*, was published with the help of MacDonagh in 1911. He wrote poetry constantly: love poems arising from a long and tormented love-affair, and mystical poetry with religious iconography, which sprang from his deep religious faith. Plunkett was co-founder of the Irish Theatre and was involved in *The Irish Review*, a monthly journal of art, literature and science founded in 1911 by Thomas MacDonagh and others. By 1913 the journal was struggling and Plunkett took over ownership and became editor. With the charged political atmosphere, *The Irish Review* became more political, and Plunkett invited contributions from James Connolly, Roger Casement and others who were gathering together in readiness for the Irish revolution.

Sympathetic to the workers during the 1913 Lockout, he was at the same time emerging as a leader in the nationalist movement, building up contacts with like-minded activists and idealists and planning the future of the Irish Volunteers. Plunkett, a brilliant military strategist, was director of military operations in the Irish Volunteers' central executive. He drilled the Irish Volunteers in Larkfield Park in Kimmage, which was owned by his family, and brought Michael Collins to his side. His fascination with radio was also to prove invaluable during Easter Week.

1915 found Plunkett, alongside Roger Casement, in Germany engaged in complicated negotiations with the German government, with the purpose of shipping arms to Ireland for a strike against Britain. He made the arduous journey alone across Spain and Italy and north through Switzerland, in what was a cloak-and-dagger adventure, all the time struggling with severe ill-health. As part of the same mission, and by then very ill, he undertook another journey to New York to connect with John Devoy, a key figure in the Irish-American nationalist organisation, Clan na Gael. Plunkett was at the centre of the planning of the Easter Rising and succeeded, along with Pearse and Seán MacDermott, in convincing James Connolly to join with them. By Easter 1916 Plunkett was a dying man and came straight from his hospital bed to carry out his commitments to the Rising. He and Grace Gifford postponed their marriage, which was to have taken place on Easter Sunday. His courage and leadership were noted by all who came in contact with him during the gruelling days and nights under fire in the General Post Office, much of which time he was forced by illness to spend lying down.

After the surrender the General Post Office was evacuated and Plunkett spent a long night lying in the open outside the Rotunda, followed by a march to Richmond Barracks. Condemned to death for his part in the Rising and his signature on the Proclamation, Joseph Plunkett was then imprisoned in Kilmainham Jail and ordered to be shot at dawn on 4 May 1916. Grace and he were married in his prison cell the night before his execution.

I SEE HIS BLOOD UPON THE ROSE

I see his blood upon the rose
And in the stars the glory of his eyes,
His body gleams amid eternal snows,
His tears fall from the skies.

I see his face in every flower;
The thunder and the singing of the birds
Are but his voice—and carven by his power
Rocks are his written words.

All pathways by his feet are worn,
His strong heart stirs the ever-beating sea,
His crown of thorns is twined with every thorn,
His cross is every tree.

THE LITTLE BLACK ROSE
SHALL BE RED AT LAST

Because we share our sorrows and our joys
And all your dear and intimate thoughts are mine
We shall not fear the trumpets and the noise
Of battle, for we know our dreams divine,
And when my heart is pillowed on your heart
And ebb and flowing of their passionate flood
Shall beat in concord love through every part
Of brain and body—when at last the blood
O'erleaps the final barrier to find
Only one source wherein to spend its strength.
And we two lovers, long but one in mind
And soul, are made one only flesh at length;
Praise God if this my blood fulfils the doom
When you, dark rose, shall redden into bloom.

THE STARS SANG IN GOD'S GARDEN

The stars sang in God's garden;
The stars are the birds of God;
The night-time is God's harvest,
Its fruits are the words of God.

God ploughed His fields at morning,
God sowed His seed at noon,
God reaped and gathered in His corn
With the rising of the moon.

The sun rose up at midnight,
The sun rose red as blood,
It showed the Reaper, the dead Christ,
Upon His cross of wood.

For many live that one may die,
And one must die that many live—
The stars are silent in the sky
Lest my poor songs be fugitive.

THIS HERITAGE TO THE RACE OF KINGS

This heritage to the race of kings
Their children and their children's seed
Have wrought their prophecies in deed
Of terrible and splendid things.

The hands that fought, the hearts that broke
In old immortal tragedies,
These have not failed beneath the skies,
Their children's heads refuse the yoke.

And still their hands shall guard the sod
That holds their father's funeral urn,
Still shall their hearts volcanic burn
With anger of the sons of God.

No alien sword shall earn as wage
The entail of their blood and tears,
No shameful price for peaceful years
Shall ever part this heritage.

THE DARK WAY

Rougher than Death the road I choose
Yet shall my feet not walk astray,
Though dark, my way I shall not lose
For this way is the darkest way.

Set but a limit to the loss
And something shall at last abide
The blood-stained beams that form the cross
The thorns that crown the crucified;

But who shall lose all things in One,
Shut out from heaven and the pit
Shall lose the darkness and the sun
The finite and the infinite;

And who shall see in one small flower
The chariots and the thrones of might
Shall be in peril from that hour
Of blindness and the endless night;

And who shall hear in one short name
Apocalyptic thunders seven
His heart shall flicker like a flame
'Twixt hell's gates and the gates of heaven.

For I have seen your body's grace,
The miracle of the flowering rod,
And in the beauty of your face,
The glory of the face of God,

And I have heard the thunderous roll
Clamour from heights of prophecy
Your splendid name, and from my soul
Uprose the clouds of minstrelsy.

Now I have chosen in the dark
The desolate way to walk alone
Yet strive to keep alive one spark
Of your known grace and grace unknown.

And when I leave you lest my love
Should seal your spirit's ark with clay,
Spread your bright wings, O shining dove,—
But my way is the darkest way.

TO GRACE

On the Morning of her Christening,
April 7th, 1916

The powerful words that from my heart
Alive and throbbing leap and sing
Shall bind the dragon's jaws apart
Or bring you back a vanished spring;
They shall unseal and seal again
The fount of wisdom's awful flow,
So this one guerdon they shall gain
That your wild beauty still they show.

The joy of Spring leaps from your eyes,
The strength of dragons in your hair,
In your young soul we still surprise
The secret wisdom flowing there;
But never word shall speak or sing
Inadequate music where above
Your burning heart now spreads its wing
In the wild beauty of your Love.

WHEN

THE DAWN

IS COME

GEORGE WILLIAM
RUSSELL (Æ)
(1867—1935)

George Russell, or Æ (his pen name came from the mystical idea of 'aeon'), was a poet, a mystic, a painter and a social organiser. His ideas and his personality helped to shape and stimulate the cultural life of Ireland in the decades around the late nineteenth and early twentieth centuries. Born a Presbyterian in Lurgan, County Armagh, he grew up in Dublin and from his youth he was committed to independence for Ireland. It was while attending the Dublin Metropolitan School of Art that he met WB Yeats, who became a lifelong friend. In order to earn a living, Æ spent a decade working as a cashier in Pim's, a department store in South Great George's Street, but he was better known as a large-minded and gentle intellectual at the centre of the Irish literary revival in Dublin.

Artists, writers and activists gathered round him in his home at 17 Rathgar Avenue in Dublin, where he held weekly tea parties, making him the centre of a mosaic of the creative minds of the day. WB Yeats, James Stephens, Padraic and Mary Colum, Thomas MacDonagh and Dermot O'Byrne were part of his circle. He generously encouraged young writers – people as diverse as James Joyce, Francis Ledwidge, and later Austin Clarke. His own *Collected Poems* was published in 1913. Æ was a prolific painter; Hugh Lane acquired several of his paintings for his collection. He had a deep interest in mysticism, about which he wrote extensively, and was a member of Madame Blavatsky's Theosophical Society.

For an impassioned idealist and literary man, Æ was blessed with practical organisational skills, and at Yeats's behest, Horace Plunkett appointed him as director of the Irish Agricultural Organisation Society (IAOS), a cooperative movement for the farming community. In the course of his work, the indefatigable Æ visited every county in Ireland, setting up creameries and banks, addressing meetings and promoting the idea of a new social order. He edited and wrote for *The Irish Homestead*, the journal of the IAOS, where poems and stories were published alongside articles on all aspects of farming and agriculture. Illustrations were often supplied from paintings by Æ. Three stories by James Joyce were first printed in *The Irish Homestead*, a whole decade before they were published as part of *Dubliners*. The workers' strike and the Great Lockout drew a passionate response from Æ as he publicly lambasted William Martin Murphy during the Dublin Lockout in 1913.

Æ's response to the Easter Rising was one of admiration for the leaders and of hope for an independent and self-sufficient Ireland. He was unaware of the events in Dublin in Easter week 1916 as he was in County Clare visiting his friend, the genealogist Edward MacLysaght, and painting in the woods at Raheen.

Much of Æ's poetic work is mystical and idealistic, but his capacity to engage with the realities of life and his love for his country brought forth a clarity of thought which inspired his best work. The poems included here are examples of his character as sympathetic observer of the Rising.

A LEADER

Though your eyes with tears were blind,
Pain upon the path you trod:
Well we knew, the hosts behind,
Voice and shining of a god.

For your darkness was our day:
Signal fires, your pains untold
Lit us on our wandering way
To the mystic heart of gold.

Naught we knew of the high land,
Beauty burning in its spheres;
Sorrow we could understand
And the mystery told in tears.

ON BEHALF OF SOME IRISHMEN NOT FOLLOWERS OF TRADITION

They call us aliens, we are told,
Because our wayward visions stray
From that dim banner they unfold,
The dreams of worn-out yesterday.
The sum of all the past is theirs,
The creeds, the deeds, the fame, the name,
Whose death-created glory flares
And dims the spark of living flame.
They weave the necromancer's spell,
And burst the graves where martyrs slept,
Their ancient story to retell,
Renewing tears the dead have wept.
And they would have us join their dirge,
This worship of an extinct fire
In which they drift beyond the verge
Where races all outworn expire.
The worship of the dead is not
A worship that our hearts allow,
Though every famous shade were wrought
With woven thorns above the brow.
We fling our answer back in scorn:

'We are less children of this clime
Than of some nation yet unborn
Or empire in the womb of time.
We hold the Ireland in the heart
More than the land our eyes have seen,
And love the goal for which we start
More than the tale of what has been.'
The generations as they rise
May live the life men lived before,
Still hold the thought once held as wise,
Go in and out by the same door.
We leave the easy peace it brings:
The few we are shall still unite
In fealty to unseen kings
Or unimaginable light.
We would no Irish sign efface,
But yet our lips would gladlier hail
The firstborn of the Coming Race
Than the last splendour of the Gael.
No blazoned banner we unfold—
One charge alone we give to youth,
Against the sceptred myth to hold
The golden heresy of truth.

SALUTATION

To the Memory of Some I Knew Who Are Dead
and Who Loved Ireland

Their dream had left me numb and cold,
But yet my spirit rose in pride,
Refashioning in burnished gold
The images of those who died
Or were shut in the penal cell.
Here's to you, Pearse, your dream not mine,
But yet the thought for this you fell
Has turned life's waters into wine.

I listened to high talk from you,
Thomas MacDonagh, and it seemed
The words were idle, but they grew
To nobleness by death redeemed.
Life cannot utter words more great
Than life may meet by sacrifice:
High words were equalled by high fate,
You paid the price. You paid the price.

The hope lives on age after age
Earth with its beauty might be won
For labour as a heritage.
For this has Ireland lost a son.
This hope unto a flame to fan
Men have put life by with a smile.
Here's to you, Connolly, my man,
Who cast the last torch on the pile.

Here's to the women of our blood
Stood by them in the fiery hour,
Rapt lest some weakness in their mood
Rob manhood of a single power.
You, brave on such a hope forlorn,
Who smiled through crack of shot and shell,
Though the world cry on you in scorn,
Here's to you, Constance, in your cell.

Here's to you men I never met,
Yet hope to meet behind the veil,
Thronged on some starry parapet
That looks down upon Innisfail,
And see the confluence of dreams
That clashed together in our night,
One river born from many streams,
Roll in one blaze of blinding light.

CONTINUITY

No sign is made while empires pass.
The flowers and stars are still His care,
The constellations hid in grass,
The golden miracles in air.

Life in an instant will be rent
Where death is glittering blind and wild—
The Heavenly Brooding is intent
To that last instant on Its child.

It breathes the glow in brain and heart,
Life is made magical. Until
Body and spirit are apart
The Everlasting works Its will.

In that wild orchid that your feet
In their next falling shall destroy,
Minute and passionate and sweet
The Mighty Master holds His joy.

Though the crushed jewels droop and fade
The Artist's labours will not cease,
And of the ruins shall be made
Some yet more lovely masterpiece.

FRANCIS LEDWIDGE

(1887—1917)

Francis Ledwidge was a poet, a patriot and a soldier. Like many young Irishmen of his time, his life had all the poignancy of those who were born to die young far from home, in the slaughter of the Great War. His short life's journey began near Slane in rural County Meath, close to the great passage tombs of the Boyne Valley. He was formed by the rural, pastoral countryside of the landscape and by his love for his country. One of nine children, he was brought up by his widowed mother, who worked in the fields to support her family. Ledwidge's early years were typical of many in the Ireland of his day, where further education was out of the question and work was hard to find. He worked on farms, on the roads and on a newspaper in Navan while writing poetry all the while, poetry that celebrated the mood and colour of the months and seasons:

Broom out the floor now, lay the fender by,
And plant this bee-sucked bough of woodbine
  there,
And let the window down.

From the poem 'June'.

He was befriended by Lord Dunsany, a local landowner who had literary interests and who generously promoted Ledwidge's work. Dunsany introduced him to Æ, Thomas MacDonagh, Katharine Tynan and other literary figures of the day. Ledwidge was a keen nationalist; he attended Irish classes and founded a branch of the Irish Volunteers in Navan. On the outbreak of the Great War, he was vehemently against John Redmond's appeal to join Irish regiments in support of the British Army, so it came as a great surprise to his friends, and made for much speculation, when he enlisted for the war effort. He later stated adamantly that he could not stand aside while others defended Ireland's freedom.

Some believe that the reason for his joining up was the loss of his first love, a loss that he never recovered from and which informed much of his poetry. 'I'm wild for wandering to the far-off places/Since one forsook me whom I held most dear,' he wrote in June 1914, in 'After My Last Song'. As it was, he enlisted with the Royal Inniskilling Fusiliers and first saw action in Gallipoli. His first book of poems, *Songs of the Fields*, was published as he was enduring a bitter winter in the snow in Serbia. Even in the madness of war, Ledwidge never ceased to write, and after his death two further collections, *Songs of Peace* (1917) and *Last Songs* (1918), were seen through the press by Dunsany.

There is little doubt that were Francis Ledwidge in Ireland at the time of the Easter Rising, he would have been part of that historic event. His poem 'Ireland' says as much:

> It is my grief your voice I couldn't hear
> > In such a distant clime.

As it was, he was hospitalised in Manchester over Easter 1916 when word of the Rising took him by complete surprise. The shocking news of the executions that followed, and the death of Thomas MacDonagh, a personal friend, were especially painful to him and inspired his best-loved poem, which begins: 'He shall not hear the bittern cry...'. The haunting quality of the verse is due in part to the use of the Gaelic mode of internal rhyme so beloved of Thomas MacDonagh in his own work.

In December 1916, having been at home on leave, Ledwidge was back in the war, posted to the

Western Front. He was engaged in road-building near the village of Boezinge in Belgium, during the Third Battle of Ypres, when a shell exploded, killing him and five others. Francis Ledwidge is buried in Artillery Wood Military Cemetery in Belgium. He is remembered also at The Island of Ireland Peace Park at Messines in Belgium, with lines from his poem 'Soliloquy' inscribed on a plaque.

It is too late now to retrieve
A fallen dream, too late to grieve
A name unmade, but not too late
To thank the gods for what is great;
A keen-edged sword, a soldier's heart,
Is greater than a poet's art.
And greater than a poet's fame
A little grave that has no name,
Whence honour turns away in shame.

The home of Francis Ledwidge in Janeville, near Slane, County Meath, is a museum to his memory.

THOMAS MACDONAGH

He shall not hear the bittern cry
In the wild sky, where he is lain,
Nor voices of the sweeter birds
Above the wailing of the rain.

Nor shall he know when loud March blows
Thro' slanting snows her fanfare shrill,
Blowing to flame the golden cup
Of many an upset daffodil.

And when the Dark Cow leaves the moor,
And pastures poor with greedy weeds,
Perhaps he'll hear her low at morn
Lifting her horn in pleasant meads.

IRELAND

I called you by sweet names by wood and linn,
You answered not because my voice was new,
And you were listening for the hounds of Finn
       And the long hosts of Lugh.

And so, I came unto a windy height
And cried my sorrow, but you heard no wind,
For you were listening to small ships in flight,
       And the wail on hills behind.

And then I left you, wandering the war
Armed with will, from distant goal to goal,
To find you at the last free as of yore,
       Or die to save your soul.

And then you called to us from far and near
To bring your crown from out the deeps of time.
It is my grief your voice I couldn't hear
       In such a distant clime.

TO MRS JOSEPH PLUNKETT

You shall not lack our little praise
If such can win your fair renown.
The halcyon of your lost days
We shall replace with living crown.

We see you not as one of us
Who so lament each little thing.
You profit more by honest loss,
Who lost so much, than song can sing.

This you have lost, a heart which bore
An ideal love, an ideal shame,
And earned this thing, for evermore
A noble and a splendid name.

Written on leave in Derry, December 1916

THE DEAD KINGS

All the dead kings came to me
At Rosnaree, where I was dreaming.
A few stars glimmered through the morn,
And down the thorn the dews were streaming.

And every dead king had a story
Of ancient glory, sweetly told.
It was too early for the lark,
But the starry dark had tints of gold.

I listened to the sorrows three
Of that Éire passed into song.
A cock crowed near a hazel croft,
And up aloft dim larks winged strong.

And I, too, told the kings a story
Of later glory, her fourth sorrow:
There was a sound like moving shields
In high green fields and the lowland furrow.

And one said: 'We who yet are kings
Have heard these things lamenting inly.'
Sweet music flowed from many a bill
And on the hill the morn stood queenly.

And one said: 'Over is the singing,
And bell bough ringing, whence we come;
With heavy hearts we'll tread the shadows,
In honey meadows birds are dumb.'

And one said: 'Since the poets perished
And all they cherished in the way,
Their thoughts unsung, like petal showers
Inflame the hours of blue and grey.'

And one said: 'A loud tramp of men
We'll hear again at Rosnaree.'
A bomb burst near me where I lay.
I woke, 'twas day in Picardy.

France, January 1917

O'CONNELL STREET

A noble failure is not vain,
But hath a victory its own.
A bright delectance from the slain
Is down the generations thrown.

And, more than Beauty understands,
Has made her lovelier here, it seems.
I see white ships that crowd her strands,
For mine are all the dead men's dreams.

France, June 1917

A SOLDIER'S GRAVE

Then in the lull of midnight, gentle arms
Lifted him slowly down the slopes of death,
Lest he should hear again the mad alarms
Of battle, dying moans, and painful breath.

And where the earth was soft for flowers we made
A grave for him that he might better rest.
So, Spring shall come and leave it sweet arrayed,
And there the lark shall turn her dewy nest.

WILLIAM BUTLER
YEATS
(1865-1939)

WB Yeats, poet, dramatist, writer, was a towering figure in the cultural life of Ireland at the time of the Easter Rising in 1916.

He was born in Dublin into a Protestant family in 1865, the son of the artist John Butler Yeats and his wife Susan Pollexfen. Yeats's forebears on his father's side were Protestant clergymen and on his mother's were Sligo merchants. His brother Jack B Yeats became Ireland's greatest painter of the twentieth century, and his sisters, Elizabeth and Susan, were engaged in many artistic enterprises and were the founders of The Cuala Press.

For the Yeats children, their childhood world was Sligo where they spent their summers, and for the young poet, it was a dreamworld of fairytales, legends and folklore. His early writings were peopled by the heroes and heroines of the great myths of the Celts. Place names such as Ben Bulben, Knocknarea, Glencar found their way into his poetry so that the landscape came to be celebrated as that part of Ireland known as 'The Yeats Country'.

For his formal schooling, Yeats attended High School in Dublin and he studied art at the Metropolitan School of Art, where he and George Russell (Æ) began what was to be a lifelong friendship.

His friendship with the old Fenian John O'Leary led him into nationalism, and under his influence and that of Maud Gonne Yeats became involved with republicanism in the 1890s. He had first met Maud Gonne in London in 1889. The daughter of a British Army major at the Curragh, County Kildare, Maud Gonne was beautiful and unconventional; she was to be muse, inspiration and the embodiment of Ireland itself in Yeats's work. Her marriage to Major John MacBride in 1903 shocked and saddened him. The love poems he wrote to her are haunting, filled with symbolism, longing and sadness.

WB Yeats was at the heart of the Irish literary revival. He promoted the idea of a distinctive literature so that Irish people would realise their own Irish spiritual and cultural heritage. He founded Irish literary societies in London and Dublin. He lectured frequently on art and culture and their connection with nationalism. He encouraged younger poets: his advice to Thomas MacDonagh was to read and translate from the Irish in order to experience the Irish mode of expression. He recognised the genius of John Millington Synge and sent him to the Aran Islands in order to learn the dialect and speech of the people. The idea of a national theatre became a reality through Yeats's friendship with Lady Gregory, and his passion for drama became realised through his own plays, among them *The Countess Cathleen* and *On Baile's Strand*. He was producer-manager of the Abbey Theatre which opened in 1904.

Lady Gregory's estate, Coole Park in south County Galway, with its library, its lake and its seven woods, was a haven and an inspiration for Yeats. So too was the towerhouse Thoor Ballylee nearby, which Yeats and his wife, George Hyde-Lees, restored and lived in for several summers and which Yeats referred to as 'the permanent symbol' of his work.

In 1923 WB Yeats was awarded the Nobel Prize for Literature, which he accepted as an honour for Ireland. He died in 1939 at Roquebrune in France and his body was reinterred at Drumcliffe Churchyard, Sligo, in 1948.

Despite being detached from nationalist politics, by Easter 1916 Yeats found beauty in the events of that time, and the poems that he was inspired to write contributed to the aura of momentous history surrounding the Rising.

As well as being the greatest Irish poet of the twentieth century, Yeats was an intellectual and artistic reformer who shaped a vision of Ireland for the Irish people, the likes of which no political leader could ever have achieved.

EASTER 1916

I have met them at close of day
Coming with vivid faces
From counter or desk among grey
Eighteenth-century houses.
I have passed with a nod of the head
Or polite meaningless words,
Or have lingered awhile and said
Polite meaningless words,
And thought before I had done
Of a mocking tale or a gibe
To please a companion
Around the fire at the club,
Being certain that they and I
But lived where motley is worn:
All changed, changed utterly:
A terrible beauty is born.

That woman's days were spent
In ignorant good-will,
Her nights in argument
Until her voice grew shrill.
What voice more sweet than hers
When, young and beautiful,
She rode to harriers?
This man had kept a school
And rode our wingèd horse;
This other his helper and friend
Was coming into his force;
He might have won fame in the end,
So sensitive his nature seemed,
So daring and sweet his thought.
This other man I had dreamed
A drunken, vainglorious lout.
He had done most bitter wrong
To some who are near my heart,
Yet I number him in the song;
He, too, has resigned his part
In the casual comedy;
He, too, has been changed in his turn,
Transformed utterly:
A terrible beauty is born.

Hearts with one purpose alone
Through summer and winter seem
Enchanted to a stone
To trouble the living stream.
The horse that comes from the road,
The rider, the birds that range
From cloud to tumbling cloud,
Minute by minute they change;
A shadow of cloud on the stream
Changes minute by minute;
A horse-hoof slides on the brim,
And a horse plashes within it;
The long-legged moor-hens dive,
And hens to moor-cocks call;
Minute by minute they live:
The stone's in the midst of all.

Too long a sacrifice
Can make a stone of the heart.
O when may it suffice?
That is Heaven's part, our part
To murmur name upon name,
As a mother names her child
When sleep at last has come
On limbs that had run wild.
What is it but nightfall?
No, no, not night but death;
Was it needless death after all?
For England may keep faith
For all that is done and said.
We know their dream; enough
To know they dreamed and are dead;
And what if excess of love
Bewildered them till they died?
I write it out in a verse—
MacDonagh and MacBride
And Connolly and Pearse
Now and in time to be,
Wherever green is worn,
Are changed, changed utterly:
A terrible beauty is born.

September 25, 1916

SIXTEEN DEAD MEN

O but we talked at large before
The sixteen men were shot,
But who can talk of give and take,
What should be and what not
While those dead men are loitering there
To stir the boiling pot?

You say that we should still the land
Till Germany's overcome;
But who is there to argue that
Now Pearse is deaf and dumb?
And is their logic to outweigh
MacDonagh's bony thumb?

How could you dream they'd listen
That have an ear alone
For those new comrades they have found,
Lord Edward and Wolfe Tone,
Or meddle with our give and take
That converse bone to bone?

THE ROSE TREE

'O words are lightly spoken,'
Said Pearse to Connolly,
'Maybe a breath of politic words
Has withered our Rose Tree;
Or maybe but a wind that blows
Across the bitter sea.'

'It needs to be but watered,'
James Connolly replied,
'To make the green come out again
And spread on every side,
And shake the blossom from the bud
To be the garden's pride.'

'But where can we draw water,'
Said Pearse to Connolly,
'When all the wells are parched away?
O plain as plain can be
There's nothing but our own red blood
Can make a right Rose Tree.'

IN MEMORY OF
EVA GORE-BOOTH
AND CON MARKIEWICZ

The light of evening, Lissadell,
Great windows open to the south,
Two girls in silk kimonos, both
Beautiful, one a gazelle.
But a raving autumn shears
Blossom from the summer's wreath;
The older is condemned to death,
Pardoned, drags out lonely years
Conspiring among the ignorant.
I know not what the younger dreams —
Some vague Utopia — and she seems,
When withered old and skeleton-gaunt,
An image of such politics.
Many a time I think to seek
One or the other out and speak
Of that old Georgian mansion, mix
Pictures of the mind, recall
That table and the talk of youth,
Two girls in silk kimonos, both
Beautiful, one a gazelle.

Dear shadows, now you know it all,
All the folly of a fight
With a common wrong or right.
The innocent and the beautiful
Have no enemy but time;
Arise and bid me strike a match
And strike another till time catch;
Should the conflagration climb,
Run till all the sages know.
We the great gazebo built,
They convicted us of guilt;
Bid me strike a match and blow.

October 1927

AFTERMATH

& REQUIEM

EVA GORE-BOOTH

(1870-1926)

Eva Gore-Booth was born into a privileged background at Lissadell in County Sligo. Like her better-known sister, Constance (later Countess Markievicz), she grew up to be a rebel, a campaigner and a feminist, though unlike Constance, she deplored militancy and was a committed pacifist all her life. Growing up in Sligo, even within the walls of a great estate, she was painfully aware of the inequalities of life. Eva witnessed famine in the locality in the late 1870s, the struggles of the Land League and the injustices caused by the landlord system. This awareness was to become the driving force of her life's work and would lead her to devote her life to trade-unionism and the suffragette movement. Eva Gore-Booth was a poet of some consequence. Her work was admired by WB Yeats, whom she first met in 1894, and they were to form a lasting friendship.

Eva was in London, where she had settled, when she heard news of the 1916 Rising and she travelled immediately to Dublin. Here the committed pacifist found that her sister, Constance, had led a garrison of fighting men and had held the College of Surgeons in St Stephen's Green. Her sister's imprisonment and death sentence caused Eva agony, and she was grief-stricken at the suffering of the people, the loss of life and the ruin of Dublin. The poems she wrote over the course of those events have startling immediacy and were inspired by the people she knew. Her friend Francis Sheehy-Skeffington, a pacifist like herself, was brutally murdered during the week of the Rising, and his death compounded the horror of the executions of the leaders. On her return to London, Eva flung herself into the campaign for the reprieve of Roger Casement, who was sentenced to death on charges of high treason for his part in the unsuccessful gunrunning from Germany. He was subsequently hanged in Pentonville Prison in August 1916.

Eva Gore-Booth died in London in 1926 after a long illness, cared for by her lifelong companion, Esther Roper, who was her literary executor.

HEROIC DEATH, 1916

No man shall deck their resting-place with flowers;
Behind a prison wall they stood to die,
Yet in those flowerless tragic graves of ours
Buried, the broken dreams of Ireland lie.

No cairn-heaped mound on a high windy hill
With Irish earth the hero's heart enfolds,
But a burning grave at Pentonville,
The broken heart of Ireland holds.

Ah! ye who slay the body, how man's soul
Rises above your hatred and your scorns—
All flowers fade as the years onward roll,
Theirs is the deathless wreath—a crown of thorns.

EASTER WEEK

Grief for the noble dead
Of one who did not share their strife,
And mourned that any blood was shed,
Yet felt the broken glory of their state,
Their strange heroic questioning of Fate
Ribbon with gold the rags of this our life.

COMRADES

To Con (Constance Markievicz)

The peaceful night that round me flows,
  Breaks through your iron prison doors,
Free through the world your spirit goes,
  Forbidden hands are clasping yours.

The wind is our confederate,
  The night has left her doors ajar,
We meet beyond earth's barrèd gate,
  Where all the world's wild rebels are.

FRANCIS SHEEHY-SKEFFINGTON

Dublin, April 26, 1916

No green and poisonous laurel wreath shall shade
  His brow, who dealt no death in any strife,
Crown him with olive who was not afraid
  To join the desolate unarmed ranks of life.

Who did not fear to die, yet feared to slay,
  A leader in the war that shall end war,
Unarmed he stood in ruthless Empire's way,
  Unarmed he stands on Acheron's lost shore.

Yet not alone, nor all unrecognized,
  For at his side does that scorned Dreamer stand,
Who in the Olive Garden agonized,
  Whose kingdom yet shall come in every land,

When driven men, who fight and hate and kill
  To order, shall let all their weapons fall,
And know that kindly freedom of the will
  That holds no other human will in thrall.

ROGER CASEMENT

I dream of one who is dead,
As the forms of green trees float and fall in the
   water,
The dreams float and fall in my mind.

I dream of him wandering in a far land,
I dream of him bringing hope to the hopeless,
I dream of him bringing light to the blind.

I dream of him hearing the voice,
The bitter cry of Kathleen ni Houlighaun
On the salt Atlantic wind.

I dream of the hatred of men,
Their lies against him who knew nothing of lying,
Nor was there fear in his mind.

I dream of our hopes and fears,
The long bitter struggle of the broken-hearted,
With hearts that were poisoned and hard.

I dream of the peace in his soul,
And the early morning hush on the grave of a hero
In the desolate prison yard.

I dream of the death that he died,
For the sake of God and Kathleen ni Houlighaun,
Yea, for Love and the Voice on the Wind.

I dream of one who is dead,
Above dreams that float and fall in the water
A new star shines in my mind.

DERMOT O'BYRNE
(SIR ARNOLD BAX)
(1883 — 1953)

Dermot O'Byrne was the pseudonym adopted by Sir Arnold Bax, an English composer of classical music, a poet and writer. At the age of eighteen, he discovered the poetry of WB Yeats, fell in love with Ireland and made his first visit there in 1901. Some of his music, such as the symphony *The Garden of Fand*, was inspired by Irish mythology. Whenever he came to Ireland, Bax took on an Irish identity as Dermot O'Byrne. He was drawn to the wild beauty of Connemara and Donegal, where he spent entire summers. He also spent long periods in Dublin, taking a house in Bushy Park, Rathgar, where he forged a deep friendship with George Russell (Æ) and his intellectual group.

Having met Pádraic Pearse in Æ's home, Bax composed a musical setting for Æ's poem 'A Leader' in homage to Pearse. In the aftermath of the Rising, he responded with an orchestral work entitled *In Memoriam Pádraig Mac Piarais* and he also wrote several poems rejoicing in the idea of Irish freedom. These were suppressed by the British censor and so were circulated privately. His affinity with Ireland and his friendship with the musician and composer Aloys Fleischmann, the pianist Tilly Fleischmann, and their family in Cork led Bax to play a significant role in Irish musical affairs. From the 1920s onwards he was a judge at the Feis Mhaitiú, an annual festival of Irish music in Cork city, and his own compositions were becoming well known to Irish audiences. Bax received many honours in his later years. He was awarded a knighthood in 1937, and in 1947 he was honoured by the Irish government in recognition of his portrayal of Ireland through his music. He died in the Fleischmann home and was buried in Cork in 1953.

A DUBLIN BALLAD – 1916

O write it up above your hearth
And troll it out to sun and moon,
To all true Irishmen on earth
Arrest and death come late or soon.

Some boy-o whistled *Ninety-eight*
One Sunday night in College Green,
And such a broth of love and hate
Was stirred ere Monday morn was late
As Dublin town had never seen.

And god-like forces shocked and shook
Through Irish hearts that lively day,
And hope it seemed no ill could brook.
Christ! for that liberty they took
There was the ancient deuce to pay!

The deuce in all his bravery,
His girth and gall grown no whit less,
He swarmed in from the fatal sea
With pomp of huge artillery
And brass and copper haughtiness.

He cracked up all the town with guns
That roared loud psalms to fire and death,
And houses hailed down granite tons
To smash our wounded underneath.

And when at last the golden bell
Of liberty was silenced,— then
He learned to shoot extremely well
At unarmed Irish gentlemen!

Ah! where were Michael and gold Moll
And Seumas and my drowsy self?
Why did fate blot us from the scroll?
Why were we left upon the shelf,

Fooling with trifles in the dark
When the light struck so wild and hard?
Sure our hearts were as good a mark
For Tommies up before the lark
At rifle practice in the yard!

Well, the last fire is trodden down,
Our dead are rotting fast in lime,
We all can sneak back into town,
Stravague about as in old time,

And stare at gaps of grey and blue
Where Lower Mount Street used to be,
And where flies hum round muck we knew
For Abbey Street and Eden Quay.

And when the devil's made us wise
Each in his own peculiar hell,
With desert hearts and drunken eyes
We're free to sentimentalize
By corners where the martyrs fell.

MARTIAL LAW IN DUBLIN

By day this sunlit citadel of death
Flashes the arrogance of your bayonets,
Sharp biting gleams that sear our pride like teeth
Of the old dragonish sowing that begets
Even to-day as dangerous a birth
As ever bristled up from ancient earth.

Also by dusk we're home at your desire
To meditate upon your iron might.
Fool, have you padlocks for our inner fire?
Are there not long deep hours before the night
Flaming with signs of Her whose solemn eyes
Make empty all your brutish masteries?

SHELLS AT ORANMORE

April, 1916

Across this threatening tranquillity
Where are but ice-ground rocks for pasturage
Strange lumps of death came shrieking from the sea,
And still the earth's cold entrails quake with rage
That such a thing could be.

Never before had such a song been sung,
Never again perhaps while ages run
Shall the old pride of rock and wind be stung
By such an insolence winged across the sun,
So mad a challenge flung!

Man, have you roused again the unruly hosts
Sprung from the stony loins of rock and shale,
The flinty propagation of stark ghosts
Peopling these harshest townlands of the Gael,
These last wind-weary coasts?

JAMES STEPHENS

(1880—1950)

James Stephens, poet and novelist, played a major part in the cultural and literary revival of the pre-Rising period. As a writer his best-known works are *The Charwoman's Daughter* and *The Crock of Gold*. A man of wide literary interests, he established *The Irish Review* in 1911 with Padraic Colum, Thomas MacDonagh and Professor David Houston. Stephens was living in Dublin at the time of the Rising where he was Registrar of The National Gallery of Ireland, and he witnessed the events of Easter week at first hand on his way to work from his home in Fitzwilliam Place. He also spent the days during the Rising walking through the streets of Dublin and keeping a journal of what he saw. This journal, an unrivalled account of the events of Easter week, was published later in 1916 as a book under the title *The Insurrection in Dublin*.

Stephens knew most of the executed leaders personally and his poem 'Spring—1916' is a memorial and elegy to the fallen, written in a romantic mode reminiscent of John Keats. He calls on the beauties of nature to immortalise the dead heroes and give courage to the future national cause.

SPRING—1916

I

Do not forget my charge, I beg of you;
That of what flowers you find, of fairest hue
And sweetest odour, you do gather those
Are best of all the best—

A fragrant rose;
A tall calm lily from the waterside;
A half-blown poppy hanging at the side
Its head of dream,
Dreaming among the corn:
Forget-me-nots that seem
As though the morn
Had tumbled down, and grew into the clay;
And buds that sway
And swing along the way,
Easing the hearts of those who pass them by
Until they find contentment—

Do not cry!
But gather buds! and, with them, greenery
Of slender branches taken from a tree
Well bannered by the Spring that saw them fall:

And you, for you are cleverest of all,
Who have slim fingers and are pitiful!
Brimming your lap with bloom that you may cull,
Will sit apart, and weave for every head
A garland of the flowers you gatheréd.

II
Be green upon their graves, O happy Spring!
For they were young and eager who are dead!
Of all things that are young, and quivering
With eager life, be they rememberéd!
They move not here! They have gone to the clay!
They cannot die again for liberty!
Be they remembered of their land for aye!
Green be their graves, and green their memory!

Fragrance and beauty come in with the green!
The ragged bushes put on sweet attire!
The birds forget how chill these airs have been!
The clouds bloom out again in limpid fire!
Blue dawns the day! blue calm lies on the lake,
And merry sounds are fitful in the thorn!
In cover green the young blackbirds awake;
They shake their wings, and sing upon the morn.

At springing of the year you came and swung
Green flags above the newly-greening earth;
Scarce were the leaves unfolded, they were young,

Nor had outgrown the wrinkles of their birth:
Comrades they thought you of their pleasant hour,
Who had but glimpsed the sun when they saw you!
Who heard your song e'er birds had singing power,
And drank your blood e'er they drank of the dew.

Then you went down! And then, and as in pain,
The Spring, affrighted, fled her leafy ways!
The clouds came to the earth in gusty rain!
And no sun shone again for many days!
And day by day they told that one was dead!
And day by day the season mourned for you!
Until that count of woe was finishéd,
And Spring remembered all was yet to do!

She came with mirth of wind and eager leaf;
With scampering feet and reaching out of wings;
She laughed among the boughs and banished grief,
And cared again for all her baby things:
Leading along the joy that has to be!
Bidding her timid buds think on the May!
And told, that Summer comes—with victory!
And told the hope that is all creatures' stay.

Go Winter now unto your own abode,
Your time is done, and Spring is conqueror!
Lift up with all your gear and take your road!
For she is here, and brings the sun with her!

Now are we born again, and now are we,
—Wintered so long beneath an icy hand!—
New-risen into life and liberty,
Because the Spring is come into our land!

III
In other lands they may,
With public joy or dole along the way,
With pomp and pageantry and loud lament
Of drums and trumpets; or with merriment
Of grateful hearts, lead into rest and sted
The nation's dead.

If we had drums and trumpets! If we had
Aught of heroic pitch, or accent glad,
To honour you—as bids tradition old—

With banners flung or draped in mournful fold,
And pacing cortège. These should we not bring
For your last journeying!

We have no drums or trumpets! Naught have we,
But some green branches taken from a tree,
And flowers that grow at large in mead and vale!

Nothing of choice have we! Nor of avail
To do you honour as our honour deems,
And as your worth beseems!

Wait, drums and trumpets, yet a little time!
All ends, and all begins! And there is chime
At last where discord was! And joy, at last,

Where woe wept out her eyes! Be not down-cast!
Here is prosperity and goodly cheer,
For life does follow death! and death is here!

IV
Joy be with us, and honour close the tale!
Now do we dip the prow, and shake the sail,
And take the wind, and bid adieu to rest!

With gladness now we re-begin the quest
That destiny commands! Though where we go,
Or guided by what star, no man doth know!

Uncharted is our course! Our hearts untried!
And we may weary e'er we take the tide,
Or make fair haven from the moaning sea.

Be ye propitious, winds of destiny!
On us at first blow not too boisterous bold!
All Ireland hath is packed into this hold!

Her hopes fly at the peak! Now at the dawn,
We sail away—Be with us Mananán!

SEÁN O'CASEY

(1880—1964)

Seán O'Casey (Seán Ó Cathasaigh), the playwright, was born John O'Casey in Dublin to a poor Church of Ireland family. O'Casey grew up in the tenements of inner-city Dublin and this background, along with the events of 1916, was to be reflected in his work, making him a major figure as an Irish dramatist. Passionate about many causes, not least social justice, he became a member of the Irish Transport and General Workers' Union (ITGWU) and as a result lost his job in the Great Northern Railway. He was later dismissed from Eason's for insubordination. With characteristic enthusiasm, O'Casey was active on all fronts of the Gaelic revival. He was a member of the Gaelic League, studied the Irish language and was a co-founder of the St Laurence O'Toole Pipe Band. O'Casey joined the Irish Citizen Army for a time and acted as Secretary before leaving after a disagreement.

Seán O'Casey and the patriot Thomas Ashe were firm friends through their shared resistance to social injustice, and O'Casey considered that Thomas Ashe had succeeded where others failed in forging links between social reform and nationalism. When Thomas Ashe was known to be dying in the Mater Hospital from the ill-treatment he received in prison, O'Casey was part of the throng that kept vigil outside. Two poems he wrote at the time were part of the avalanche of propaganda which followed the death and funeral of Ashe, events which played their part in a major change of direction in the nationalist cause.

THOMAS ASHE

I

The Children of Éireann are listening again
  To Death's sullen, sad, sombre beat of the drum;
Oppression has seized on a man amongst men,
  And an eloquent life's stricken senseless and dumb,
  While we, left behind, wait the life from your death that
    shall come!

II

In your fight to unfetter Humanity's soul,
  Your body was blazoned with scars,
To oppression you fearlessly tendered the toll,
  Removing for progress the Bolts and the Bars,
  With your hand to the Plough and your eyes on the stars.

III

On the cold seat of death now your body's enthroned.
  And your warm heart is silent and still,
For our life that is Death, your great life has atoned,
  And we feel in our hearts a swift answering thrill,
  To take up your work, all hard fallow nature to till.

IV

Here hope and Endeavour with energy braid
  Leaves of honour to garland the Dead,
Here Liberty rests with calm Courage arrayed,
  By the side of the Kingly but now passive head,
  Anointed with blood that this Hero has shed.

V

Huge Labour looks down on your battle-scarred face,
  Ignoble and noble with sweat on his brow,
Unable to fathom this soul of his race,
  Half-conscious that soon, when he springs from the Slough,
  He shall understand then, if he can't do it now!

VI

To your soul, for awhile, we all murmur, Farewell!
  And we take the Dear Gift that you gave,
For your great Life stamped out in the cold prison cell
  Shall be potent our own slavish nature to save,
  Tho' your body we leave in the drear hidden gloom of the grave.

THOMAS ASHE

(1885–1917)

One of the leaders of the 1916 Rising, Thomas Ashe led the Volunteer forces at the battle of Ashbourne in County Meath with his second-in-command, Richard Mulcahy, in what was the only fully successful engagement of the Easter Rising. He was condemned to death, with his sentence later commuted to penal servitude for life.

Thomas Ashe came from Kinard, in the Corca Dhuibhne peninsula of County Kerry. He was raised in an environment where the Gaelic ethos prevailed, and where the ideal of an independent and self-reliant Irish nation was nurtured. He also grew up immersed in the idea of resistance to the oppression perpetrated by the system of landlordism.

During his years as a school teacher in north County Dublin, Ashe was a leader in the local community, where he promoted the Irish language, became a member of the IRB and was prominent in the Irish Volunteers.

He co-founded the Black Raven Pipe Band, still in existence today. He was a social idealist who sided with the workers during the Lockout, for which he and others were threatened with expulsion from the Gaelic League.

Ashe was released from prison in England in the general amnesty of 1917. By then president of the IRB, he was again jailed for 'seditious speeches' in August 1917. Thomas Ashe went on hunger strike in order to protest at the criminalisation of political prisoners, but died due to ill-treatment. His death changed the nationalist mood and mind of Ireland overnight, a mood reflected in the press and public bodies. His funeral was a national event which caused a massive transfer of allegiance to the nationalist cause.

The poem 'Let Me Carry Your Cross for Ireland, Lord!', written in Lewes Prison after the Rising, and repeatedly reprinted after his untimely death, is in the spirit of self-sacrifice and religious feeling that was current at the time of the Easter Rising.

LET ME CARRY YOUR CROSS
FOR IRELAND, LORD!

Let me carry your Cross for Ireland, Lord!
  The hour of her trial draws near,
And the pangs and the pains of the sacrifice
  May be borne by comrades dear.
But, Lord, take me from the offering throng,
  There are many far less prepared,
Though anxious and all as they are to die
  That Ireland may be spared.

Let me carry your Cross for Ireland, Lord!
  My cares in this world are few,
And few are the tears will fall for me
  When I go on my way to You.
Spare, oh! spare to their loved ones dear
  The brother and son and sire,
That the cause we love may never die
  In the land of our heart's desire.

Let me carry your Cross for Ireland, Lord!
  Let me suffer the pain and the shame,
I bow my head to their rage and hate,
  And I take on myself the blame.
Let them do with my body whate'er they will,
  My spirit I offer to You,
That the faithful few who heard her call
  May be spared to Róisín Dubh.

Let me carry your Cross for Ireland, Lord!
  For Ireland weak with tears,
For the aged man of the clouded brow,
  And the child of the tender years;
For the empty homes of her golden plains;
  For the hopes of her future, too!
Let me carry your Cross for Ireland, Lord,
  For the cause of Róisín Dubh.

JOYCE KILMER
(1886—1918)

Joyce Kilmer was an American journalist, a lecturer and a poet. He had no Irish family connections, but as a scholar he was widely read in the literature and history of Ireland, and as a journalist his work reflected the considerable American interest in Irish affairs. Kilmer had much in common with Joseph Mary Plunkett, whom he met in New York in 1915. In Plunkett he recognised a fellow poet who shared his religious fervour and his commitment to freedom, and he was deeply affected by Plunkett's execution after the Easter Rising.

Kilmer had converted to Roman Catholicism in 1913, the year in which his volume of poetry *Trees* was published; also the year, in fact, in which his best-known poem, 'Trees', was published along with works by WB Yeats in a literary anthology. Joyce Kilmer was an influential journalist with *The New York Times* and in the Sunday magazine of that paper he wrote an extensive article about the Rising, 'Poets March in the Van of Irish Revolt', emphasising the number of poets and writers who participated in the events in Ireland. *The New York Times* covered the Easter Rising on its front page for fourteen days (until suppressed by the censor in Ireland). Kilmer's poem 'Easter Week, In Memory of Joseph Mary Plunkett' reflects how he identified with the Irish cause.

Joyce Kilmer enlisted for the war effort and was deployed in France in 1917. He was killed at the Second Battle of the Marne on 30 July 1918. The Joyce Kilmer Memorial Forest in North Carolina is dedicated to his memory.

EASTER WEEK

In Memory of Joseph Mary Plunkett

'Romantic Ireland's dead and gone,
It's with O'Leary in the grave.'
                    —W.B. Yeats.

'Romantic Ireland's dead and gone,
It's with O'Leary in the grave.'
Then, Yeats, what gave that Easter dawn
A hue so radiantly brave?

There was a rain of blood that day,
Red rain in gay blue April weather,
It blessed the earth till it gave birth
To valour thick as blooms of heather.

Romantic Ireland never dies!
O'Leary lies in fertile ground,
And songs and spears throughout the years
Rise up where patriot graves are found.

Immortal patriots newly dead
And ye that bled in bygone years,
What banners rise before your eyes?
What is the tune that greets your ears?

The young Republic's banners smile
For many a mile where troops convene.
O'Connell Street is loudly sweet
With strains of Wearing of the Green.

The soil of Ireland throbs and glows
With life that knows the hour is here
To strike again like Irishmen,
For that which Irishmen hold dear.

Lord Edward leaves his resting place
And Sarsfield's face is glad and fierce.
See Emmet leap from troubled sleep
To grasp the hand of Pádraic Pearse!

There is no rope can strangle song
And not for long death takes his toll.
No prison bars can dim the stars
Nor quicklime eat the living soul.

Romantic Ireland is not old.
For years untold her youth shall shine.
Her heart is fed on Heavenly bread,
The blood of martyrs is her wine.

JOSEPH CAMPBELL

(1879 — 1944)

Poet, scholar, artist and ardent nationalist Joseph Campbell was born in Belfast. He is the author of many of Ireland's best known and loved songs, including 'I Will Go with My Father A-Ploughing', 'My Lagan Love' and 'The Spanish Lady'. He put words to ancient Irish airs collected by the composer Herbert Hughes in his *Songs of Uladh*. 'My Lagan Love' is one of these, written to a haunting air from Donegal. Some of Campbell's verse was also set to music by Arnold Bax. Joseph Campbell's profound knowledge of and love for the old songs, traditions and music of Ulster gave them a new audience and a lasting place in the Irish repertoire.

Campbell's passion for literature and his dedication to the future of Irish culture brought him to the centre of the Irish literary revival: he taught with Pádraic Pearse in St Enda's; he gave lessons in Irish to

Joseph Mary Plunkett and associated with the literary figures of the day. He was also active in literary circles in London, where he lived for some years. On his return from London, he moved to Glencree in County Wicklow and was a founder member of the Irish Volunteers. During the Civil War, he fought on the anti-treaty side and was imprisoned in the Curragh. Disillusioned by the politics in the new Ireland, he went to New York where he founded a school of Irish studies. Joseph Campbell died in Glencree in 1944.

Campbell, a prolific poet, drew on traditional themes for much of his work. Forgotten figures of Irish life, the shepherd, the stone-cutter, the wood-gatherer, vanishing in his lifetime, are immortalised in his poems.

FIRES

The little fires that Nature lights—
The scilla's lamp, the daffodil—
She quenches, when of stormy nights
Her anger whips the hill.

The fires she lifts against the cloud—
The irised bow, the bearing tree—
She batters down with curses loud,
Nor cares that death should be.

The fires she kindles in the soul—
The poet's mood, the rebel's thought—
She cannot master, for their coal
In other mines is wrought.

THE STORM-THRUSH ON THE SHAKING TREE

The storm-thrush on the shaking tree
Shouted loud and jubilantly—
A month, and April will unfold
Her flag of green and white and gold.

MacAlla answered thrush and tree
Louder and more jubilantly—
A year, and Ireland will unfold
Her flag of green and white and gold!

DORA SIGERSON
SHORTER
(1866 — 1918)

Dora Sigerson was a poet, a sculptor and an artist who grew up in Dublin in an atmosphere where Gaelic culture and nationalism flourished. Her parents were part of a circle of scholars and artists involved in the cultural revival, and she was writing poems and ballads from a young age. Her father, Dr George Sigerson (1836–1925), was a larger-than-life character who knew and entertained all the literary figures of his time. He was a scholar and a promoter of every aspect of Gaelic culture from sports to poetry and music. The Sigerson Cup, a trophy for Gaelic football tournaments between the colleges of the National University of Ireland, was established in 1911 by George Sigerson.

Dora Sigerson married Clement Shorter, an English journalist and editor of the *Illustrated London News*, and went to live in London. Intensely patriotic, she was much anguished by the events following the Easter Rising. Her friend, the poet Katharine Tynan, believed that her death in 1918 was brought about by her overwhelming grief. Dora Sigerson Shorter wrote a collection of elegies in the aftermath of the Rising, one for each of the executed leaders. Her body was brought home to Dublin, where she was buried in Glasnevin Cemetery. She had also designed and funded the Pietà memorial to the dead of 1916, which stands in Glasnevin Cemetery to this day.

THE STAR

In memory of Patrick Pearse

I saw a dreamer, I saw a poet,
On the red battle-field fell my slow tear,
'Lover of birds and flowers, singer of gentle songs,
Dying with men of war, what do you here?'
Languid his closing eyes looked to the breaking dawn
Where the young day peeped out through prison bars,
'I on a high hill stood singing a dear old song,
'I fell to earth,' he sighed, 'grasping at stars.'

He laid him softly down, cold was his paling cheek,
Silent and chill he grew as the dead are,
But from his folded hands on to the crimson earth
Glowing and shimmering fell a great star.
Out of the heavens there came a hand raising it,
Set in the green sky for all to see,
There it shone purely bright, faithful as planets shine,
There it sung loud and sweet, 'Come, follow me.'

THE DEAD SOLDIER

In memory of Thomas Ashe

Where the sword has opened the way the man will follow.

'Look! they came, the triumphant army!
Over yon hill see their weapons peeping!'
Still I spoke not but my wheel sent turning,
I closed my eyes for my heart was weeping,
My heart was weeping for a dead soldier.

Who is he who looks towards me?
''Tis no man but a gay flag flying,'
Red was his mouth and his white brow thoughtful,
Blue his eyes—how my soul is crying,
My soul is crying for a dead soldier.

'Kneel ye down, lest your eyes should dare them,
Kneel ye down and your beads be saying.'
'Lord, on their heads Thy wrath deliver,'
This is the prayer that my lips are praying,
My heart is praying for a dead soldier.

'Best cheer the path of the men victorious,
For he is dead and his blade lies broken,
His march is far where no aid can follow,
And for his people he left no token,
He left no token, the dead soldier.'

The way of the sword a man can follow,
See the young child with his gold hair gleaming.
When falls the oak must the acorn perish?
He lifts the blade and his eyes are dreaming,
He dreams the dream of the dead soldier.

PADRAIC COLUM

(1881—1972)

Padraic Colum was born in Longford in 1881. He wrote about the Irish countryside and the way of life of the people — the remnants of an old Ireland that was fast vanishing with the new century. Among his poems, 'An Old Woman of the Roads' and 'A Cradle Song' were learned by heart by generations of schoolchildren.

Another well-loved poem by Colum is 'She Moved Through the Fair', which is set to the haunting music of an old Irish air. But even as he celebrated 'the common furniture of daily life' in his poems, Colum was a major literary figure, a playwright, a poet, an editor and critic who was prominent in the literary revival. He founded *The Irish Review* in 1911 with Thomas MacDonagh, David Houston and James Stephens. He and his wife, Mary Maguire Colum, a noted critic and writer herself, left Ireland for New York in 1914 and became part of the international literary scene.

The 1930s saw them in Paris, where James Joyce was amongst their friends.

The executions of many of their friends after the Rising caused the Colums profound grief. 'That was the last of the executions, and with it some part of our youth died,' Mary Colum noted in her memoir *Life and the Dream* when news of the execution of Roger Casement, a personal friend, reached them in New York in August 1916.

Here is Padraic Colum's lament for Roger Casement, for which he reached into the ancient Irish tradition of the *caoine* (lament), giving the words a dignity and stateliness to mourn the loss of a leader.

THE REBEL

ROGER CASEMENT

1864–1916

They have hanged Roger Casement to the tolling of a bell,
Ochone, och, ochone, ochone!
And their Smiths and their Murrays and their Cecils say
   it's well,
Ochone, och, ochone, ochone!
But there are outcast peoples to lift that spirit high,
Flayed men and breastless women who laboured fearfully,
And they will lift him, lift him for the eyes of God to see,
And it's well, after all, Roger Casement!

They've ta'en the strangled body and laid it in the pit,
Ochone, och, ochone, ochone!
And brought the stealthy fire to waste it bit by bit,
Ochone, och, ochone, ochone!
To waste that noble stature, that grave and brightening
   face
That set courtesy and kindliness in eminence of place,
But they – they'll die to dust that no poet e'er will trace,
While 'twas yours to die to fire, Roger Casement.

CANON CHARLES O'NEILL

(1887 — 1963)

Canon Charles O'Neill was parish priest of Kilcoo in County Down. He attended the first assembly of Dáil Éireann (the Parliament of the Republic of Ireland) in the Mansion House, Dublin, on 21 January 1919, a highly symbolic and historic event. As the names of the newly elected members were called out by the Ceann Comhairle, Cathal Brugha, many of them were not present, as thirty-four members were still in jail in Britain. These included Éamon de Valera, Countess Markievicz, Desmond FitzGerald, Arthur Griffith and Terence MacSwiney. Absent by choice were the twenty-six Unionist members. O'Neill was so overcome by the day's events that he was inspired to write the fine ballad 'The Foggy Dew', a rendering of the story of the 1916 Rising. It has become one of Ireland's best loved and most performed ballads. The music to which it is sung is an old Irish air collected and arranged by Carl Hardebeck.

THE FOGGY DEW

As down the glen one Easter morn
To a city fair rode I.
There Armed lines of marching men,
In squadrons passed me by.
No pipe did hum, no battle drum
Did sound its loud tattoo.
But the Angelus Bell o'er the Liffey's
Swell rang out in the foggy dew.

Right proudly high over Dublin town
They hung out the flag of war.
'Twas better to die 'neath an Irish sky,
Than at Suvla or Sud-El-Bar.
And from the plains of Royal Meath
Brave men came hurrying through,
While Britannia's Huns, with their long range guns
Sailed in through the foggy dew.

But the night fell black, and the rifles' crack,
Made perfidious Albion reel.
Through that leaden hail, seven tongues of flame,
Did shine o'er the lines of steel.
By each shining blade a prayer was said,
That to Ireland her sons be true,
And when morning broke, still the green flag shook out,
Its folds in the foggy dew.

It was England bade our wild geese go,
That small nations might be free,
But their lonely graves are by Suvla's waves
Or the fringe of the great North Sea.
Oh, had they died by Pearse's side
Or fought along with Cathal Brugha
Their graves we'd keep where the Fenians sleep,
'Neath the shroud of the foggy dew.

But the bravest fell, and the Requiem knell,
Rang mournfully and clear,
For those who died that Eastertide
In the spring time of the year
While the world did gaze, with deep amaze,
At those fearless men, but few,
Who bore the fight that freedom's light
Might shine through the foggy dew.

As back through the glen I rode again,
And my heart with grief was sore.
For I parted then with gallant men,
I ever will see no more,
And to and fro in my dreams I go,
And I'll kneel and pray for you,
For slavery fled, oh you gallant dead,
When you fell in the foggy dew.

INDEX OF FIRST LINES